INVISIBLE INK

JENNIFER SCHNEIDER

CONTENTS

CAREFUL, YELLS PIGEON

Papaya, potato, pineapple.

Soft whispers in heavy night air

Pigeon sits on damp windowsill outside well-fur-
nished market

Bright lights shine on sliced rice cakes individually
stacked and stocked in freezers

Shaved chicken breasts in cellophane line brightly lit
back wall

Fully masked, gray haired woman wrapped in dark
gray jacket, cranberry scarf, and gingham bonnet
climbs wet concrete stairs

Careful, yells Pigeon. *Don't slip!*

Slip, slap, slop.

Soft whispers in night air

I'll take your leftovers.

BLANKS

As Day Becomes Night and Night Becomes Day and
I Struggle to Fill in the Blanks for Questions of Why
We Do What We Do, I Find Solace in Silence and
Answers in the Air Between Myself and I

Morning Routines

Sirens roar, alarms ring, and bodies turn—
right, left, right again. Limbs stretch, bare soles meet
cool wood. Muscle memory moves both body and
soul from one room of four walls to the next. *Chin up*,
they say, when I say *No*. *Quiet now*, they urge, when I
say *No*. Truth emerges like dew as eyes meet eyes in
the steamy washroom mirrors. Go ahead, tell me
what type of day awaits.

First thought, best thought. Ready. Set. Go.

    1. Something wet
    2. Something dry
    3. Something special
    4. Something lost
    5. Something old
    6. Something new

7. What you see in the mirror
8. What you hear before sleep
9. First thoughts as eyes open at dawn
10. Your most prized personal trait
11. An item in your medicine cabinet
12. Something sweet
13. Your favorite color
14. Your favorite article of clothing
15. Your least favorite season
16. Synonym for strong
17. A fear
18. An item in your refrigerator
19. A reason to be hopeful
20. Something precious
21. Something comforting
22. Another word for touch
23. Another word for greet
24. Another word for hope
25. The flavor of love
26. The most beautiful site in your world
27. Something that provokes tears of joy

The day ahead may bring __1__, __2___,
even ___3___. Perhaps ___4___. If I'm
lucky, ___5__ might meet ___6____.
If I'm not, and even when it's ___15___,
and even when ___17____ sings and screams
in my eyes, ears, and soul, I think of
___12___, ___13___ blankets, and my
___14___.

Hello, ___8___. Good day, ___9___.
I am ___10___, and I am ___16___.

Made of ___7___. ___11____
and ___18____, too.
Most of all, I think of ___19___

and ___20_____. I think
of ____21___.

I count to four and inhale. Count
back as I exhale. Then lift
my chin and open my eyes, mouth,
and heart. ____23____ world. I know
not how to give in or give up. No
matter what might come, I still taste
____25__, still see __26____, and
hear__27____. Most of all,
I still believe
in ____24___.

Evening Reflections

Any thought, a worthy thought. Ready. Set. Go.

1. Eye color
2. Color of darkness
3. Another word for quiet
4. A body part (*plural*)
5. A good night greeting

Shoulders square and tighten as __1____ eyes
focus on hallway mirrors. Shades of _2__ be-
    neath lashes. Clock hands tick as lifelines
__3__. Soft whispers float overhead. The
    day's events on repeat. __4__ flick
switch as rooms darken. _5__ world.

CONNECTIVE TISSUE

We played *Connect 4* last night. Only it was *Connect 5* and called by some other name. Its title escapes me now. I envy the title's ability to flee as I remain both present and presently disoriented. The laminated gameboard rotated randomly. To the right. The left, too. I never knew which way it was going to turn. The game adopted all of the traditional rules—one color per player, proceed in clockwise formation, wait turns. Only, there was little tradition. Superficial familiarity lacked both substance and solidarity. Gravity played cruel tricks. Predictable patterns— rows and columns of monochromatic chips—turned chaotic. Four shiny reds in a row quickly turned to three blue with one red in the middle. Next, three in a row blue—standing in solidarity—rotated to form a patchwork of green, yellow, blue, and red—some chips wayward, others alone—in a rotating fashion. Turns rotated, time, too. I went through the motions, but my motions no longer mattered. I asked for mercy following norms and niceties—added a merci —yet found none.

I should have chosen another box from the shelf. There were many options. Classics such as *Life* and

Clue. *Monopoly*, too. Newcomers with familiar elements. *Smart Ass*. *Noodlers*. *Blokus*. Each wrong. I had no clue what life was any longer. Thoughts monopolized by news. News monopolized by limits and limitations. Mirrors seeking Mercy. Mirrors revealing Memory. All elements of the game. As a child, I preferred *Twister* to *Trivial Pursuit*. *Othello* to *Ouija*. Now, I crave life with fewer twists and turns. Coffee and care spill unexpectedly. Carelessly and casually, too.

Temperatures rise and what rises falls. I used to be able to visualize patterns. Count possibilities and pursue unique paths and distinguishable outcomes in advance of their fruition. Consumed apples before fully ripe. Bananas, too. Reality and ripeness both a relatable route. Now, I feel as if I am always in a reactionary zone. Table talk and teams. Red on black. Blue on green. Unsuspected alliances and unsuspecting moves. Chips drop, then scatter. Traps taunt. Play persists, too.

I cleaned the stove top in between rounds. Scrubbed at grease that secured its position— spots on the board of *Life*—long ago. Worked on the overhead hood, too. Spent a few hours scrubbing with little impact. As my fingers scraped, my eyes observed a community of ants on the floor. I must have dropped crumbs while I prepared snacks—a bowl of popcorn, a plate of veggie straws, and M&Ms. More colors than I recalled. More competition, too. Each a symbol of what once was. Memories washed in the kitchen sink and wiped with days old paper.

I thought of the many communities I'd lost touch with, and track of, over the past twelve months. Dried ink and texting trains that trailed off. Connecting the dots now an impossible task. Classrooms left at Chapter 8 of *War and Peace*. Book clubs suspended at page 84 of *The Sun Always Rises*. Stalled trains and bored bargain hunters. Bus seat companions, too.

The No. 5 bus no longer runs, yet many still wait—and sleep—at the corner of 10th and Main. A friend lost his game of Life last September. Another this past January. Just as the media released upbeat news. Trials of many kinds. Time always wins. It's too bad the kitchen drawer, the one with my needles, is a mess. Connective tissue stretches, then snaps. Translucent fibers break. Game night part of the weekly routine. I could have gone cold turkey—like the sandwiches we had for dinner last night and the night before, too—but chose to go through the motions instead. Feign cooperative play. Stop competing. Stop caring. Stop calculating. I stopped writing, too. No longer know the way nor what to say. Too many lost connections. Too many connecting options. Too many lost rounds of *Connect 4*.
Connect 5, too.

BETWEEN HERE AND THERE

Fragments of imagination—mine/theirs/ours—and memory—float in the small pockets of air between *Here and There*. Always. All crave something—chocolate, chutney, confirmation—I reach as far as my arms will stretch. Further. Particles scatter. My fingers, and their emerald green painted nails, wiggle, the silver band on my left hand looser than ever before. *Be careful* flutters in my left ear. No matter. The canvas before me is lovely. Children's hand-painted portraits, puppets that dance, butterflies that sing. Cranberries, blueberries, mangos. Soft winds, gentle honey bees. Blankets of sunshine, interlocked hands, and lemon-scented laughter. Love—*Here and There*. Now.

My right elbow cracks as granular images dodge awkward attempts to recreate and retrieve. Everything is broken. *Here. Now.* I dwell on digital substitutes—mountains of unanswered communications. Mirror carvings that defy connection. I struggle to breathe then regain, if not retrieve and retain, my composure. Casually, of course. Privately, I wonder about the difference between retrieve and retain. Retrain and retry, too. Ultimately, I accept defeat and

defer to the physical realities before me. I sit, as
gravity wishes. I retreat, as air density demands. I si-
lence in solitude, as reality recommends. Finally, I de-
cline to dance, as force and time dictate. Yet, I
continue to dream of the declining space between
Here and There.

There is a Land of raspberry-flavored warmth and
chicken broth for all souls.

Here is a Land of purchase restricted entry and ac-
cess—recipes out of reach—and bookstore copies of
chicken soup stories—stock sealed.

There is a Land of innocence and freedom without
three-digit price tags.

Here is a Land of overpriced lattes and over-pro-
cessed shelves in dollar store pantries, where inflation
races ignition, pardons are commodities, and health
care an alternate version of history.
There is a Land where texts document all histories
and where all histories are documented.

Here is a Land where zip codes serve as both lifelines
and predictors of lifetimes. Where the innocent
serve. Testimony. Time. TV.

There is a Land of unsealed codes, zippers on all
coats, and genuine ovations, where zip codes and
country IDs reflect origins and destinations rather
than outcomes, and where days are marked by the
consumption of food groups and crops curated for
fair wages and by workers of appropriate ages.

Here is a Land of dark webs and spiders. Of anony-
mous posts, digital consumption, and potent poisons

that stick and strike in silence and in spaces of silent audiences.

There is a Land where spiders and soldiers coexist in peace, of altos and sopranos and harmonies that hum of shared spaces where pop meets rap and jazz dances with all classics.

Here is a Land of Now. I see *There* in the dust that collects on the fragments that float in the small spaces beneath the plaid covers and my patchwork dreams. *There:* just out of reach. Too this. Too that. Too much *Here.* Determined, I continue to try. The air smells of soured cottage cheese, yet my fingers stretch without care. The digital clock beeps. I push past PM only to arrive, once again, at AM. The space between *Here and There* both expands and con-stricts. Casually, of course.

Here is a Land where children collect and receive beans for cocoa.

There is a Land of rocking chairs with cushions, platforms with mattresses, and faucets with clean water.

There is a Land where luck is as accessible as unluck, and the sun shines on all faces and to the same degree

There is a Land where residents of the Amazon and employees of Amazon are treated with care.

There is a Land of _1, 2, 3, 4, and/or 5__, where the sky is a source of possibility and stars line streets for all that stroll.

Here is a Land where Ebbinghaus' Forgetting curve conceals patterns of pain and power.

I do not want to forget. I want to remember. I want a Land where memory is neither contaminated nor contextualized, and truths are not tainted. Where John Lewis's good trouble is the only kind of trouble there is. Where students are not soldiers, and where soldiers are not statues. Where statutes no longer sting, and where saints sing in solidarity. Where schools are soft landings and retreats from darkness. Where light shines on all, and where the lights at the end of a tunnel is neither a train to detention nor a turnstile with a guard to the right and a trap to the left

Where Here is There

1. The color of happiness
2. The flavor of safety
3. The scent of peace
4. The taste of justice
5. The sound of freedom

Where Here and There
is a Land of _1_, _2_,
_3_, _4_, and _5_.

IN THE SPIRIT OF STUFF

Puzzle Pieces

The wood table hides under a blanket of brightly colored cardboard and stray shavings. All nine hundred and ninety-nine pieces of the one-thousand-piece puzzle. The high gloss photo on the laminated box taunts. Circus smiles, red noses, soulful elephants all under the big top. I spend the hours between eight and twelve searching for the missing piece. Under the table. In the radiator. On the floor. The dog sleeps. The kids study. The heater hums. I do not find success.

Hallmark Cards

Old greetings—birthdays, get well soon, sympathy, and holiday wishes. The signature lines are as varied as the email closings that now puncture my day at a frequency far greater than the postal mail ever did. Best, Sincerely, With gratitude, All my best, Best regards, ____. I don't know what any of them mean. I do not know why I saved them. The best is surely either in the past or yet to come. Most definitely not the present. I've taken to deleting emails, though my box is never empty. At last look, I had 42,657 unread messages in my inbox. I could spend all day, every day, for weeks on end, sorting electronic mail. Why, then, do I crave connection?

Surplus

One cabinet houses and hides seven sets of identical salt and pepper shakers. Tiny glass bottles perched on, no in, the belly of a sterling silver duck with extra-large webbed feet. Well balanced even while well out of proportion. An outcome of my one-time interaction with QVC. I had ordered a single set after a return from Boston and a visit to the Gardens. Back when travel was still friends with time. When time told stories, and stories were worth sharing. Make way for the ducklings and Beacon Hill still fresh in mind and water. The outlet sent one carton stocked with twelve. And they are as awful as they sound. Wide eyes frozen in horror. We all know ducks prefer fresh to saltwater. I never entertain, prefer, if not require, solitude like the ugly duckling. No one understands my humor. And, so, they sit. Behind the warped oak cabinet door to the left of the window. We've grown to tolerate each other. They don't quack, and I don't quibble.

Feedback Diets

As a young girl, I was fed a diet of frozen TV dinners. Salisbury steak and perfectly symmetrical heaps of mashed potatoes. I'd butter both and watch reruns of *The Price is Right*. As I grew, freezer contents changed. Lean Cuisines replaced Swanson. Tabatchnick minestrone soup swapped shelf space with Sara Lee pound cake. Tea and tabbouleh replaced tater tots and Tastykakes. Refrigerator contents changed, too. Sticks of butter became packets of ketchup and mustard swiped from open 7-11 trays. Mealtime conversation focused on calories and calculations. I was schooled on gender roles and expectations using the language of food. *The Price is Right* persisted. *Wheel of Fortune*, too. I was told I was fortunate. By the time I was eleven, I knew not to believe everything I was told.

Receipts

I should have tossed the crumpled papers but chopped salad instead. Raspberry vinaigrette over honey walnuts. The receipts, along with dozens of others, stuffed in the top right drawer. Impulse cheesecake. Late night Grub. Amazon QR codes. Insomnia calls yet the Internet always waits. Bulls eyes on me. Minutes tick as fingers click. Finds and finders everywhere. I should have turned down the covers but turned up the volume and turned off the alarm clock. Just in case. I've been afflicted with *just in case* concerns for as long as I can remember. Caught the desire for records young and never outgrew their grip. Not desire. Not Records. Not Receipts. I should have but did not.

Words

Pen meets paper as ink spills. Tightly coiled spirals of loose-leaf fibers relax, then float. Muddy puddles of blue, black, and red threads form a tapestry of raw wounds, woven of half-truths, mirror images, and dreams uttered. Barely audible. Fingers trace rows of eight-point font in paper volumes delivered weekly. Words rise as paper bound volumes meet new forms of consumption. Prohibitions and privileges lurk in the small pockets of air between us and them. I consume greedily, then produce new batches of words for further consumption. Strings of syllables, most linger slightly below my stream of consciousness. Destination unknown, I wonder who I am and why I write. As locks turn right and evening routines press, I repeat. I am an author. An author, I am. Play with, on, and of words. Puncture the silence that blankets minds.

I am an Author of words _No one / Strangers / Only I / Many / Too many / _______ read(s).

I SHOULD HAVE

I chose to languish—stocking slow burning
    candles and Dum Dum lollipop suckers
    by the dozen—but should have listened.
I should have traded baseball cards, but
    traded stocks instead.
I should have collected late-night jokes and
    half-squeezed lemons, but chose leavened
    bread and buttered biscuits instead.
I should have touched his right cheek, but
    tousled his remaining hair instead.
I should have returned the pleasantry, but re-
    turned the stare instead.
I should have resisted temptation, but chose
    to tempt fate instead.
I should have painted bedroom walls lilac,
    but painted beds of nails violet instead.
I should have sprinkled sugar, but sprinkled
    salt instead.
I should have consumed macaroni and
    cheese, but chose macaroons and
    Madeira instead.
I should have counted coins, but counted
    horses instead.
I should have picked flowers—daisies, daf-

fodils, roses, but picked dryer lint and
    fights instead.
I should have calculated time left, but calcu-
    lated time spent instead.
I should have sorted laundry, but sorted lip-
    sticks tubes--glossy, matte, sheen
        —instead.
I should have. I could have. I did not.

THINGS CALLED MUGS

1. A word for a drinking vessel stored in your kitchen cabinet.
2. A word that describes the surface of a morning coffee mug.
3. The color of an item stored in your kitchen cupboard.

4. A word that describes your fingers..
5. A word that describes your eyes.
6. A price less than $9.99. *Any non-whole dollar amount.*

7. A destination. *Anywhere other than home. Proper noun.*
8. A season.
9. An admired songwriter for/from the present.

10. A favored songwriter for/from the past.
11. A songwriter for/from the future.
12. A form of favored top level clothing. *Plural.*

13. A form of favored bottom half clothing. *Plural.*
14. Item in a kitchen sink. *Plural.*
15. Item in a kitchen drawer. *Plural.*

I grabbed it this morning, my __1__. Its __2__ __3__ exterior cool to the touch. My __4__ fingers fumble as my __5_ eyes blink. Purchased for __6__ when visiting __7__. Last __8__. I have a photo, taken as my left-hand cupped small coins—some shiny, most not—change from the transaction—and my right hand gripped the cup. Voices: Stop. Stand still. Smile. Say cheese. Don't blink. Lights flashed. Stray bolts of lighting, too. Perhaps, I imagined the spark. I saw stars although my watch ticked high-noon. Fireflies danced in small pockets of dewy air just beyond my lashes.

I always blink. Then. Now. Today. Barely able to control and confine arms that flail, legs that buckle, and complexions that always turn sallow. Eyes, no different. Pockets well of salt and sadness, and easily betray all efforts to stifle songs of sorrow and serendipity. Lyrics linger. __9___ and __10__. __11__, too.

The radio dial turns right as volume fills the empty room. To and from its furthest dust-filled corners. Parched lips and dry throat consume hot liquids, hot news, hot air. Heat always rises. The clock's second hand pulses as does the organ called the heart, concealed under layers of secondhand __12__ and __13__ painting a picture of a life pureed. Derivative skins, as well. Steamed squash, boiled carrots, melted ice cream. The freezer shut down. Just last week. On Tuesday. Long before its predicted life span. Expiration dates notwithstanding. All flavors diluted due to days being no longer distinguishable from those prior.

And those yet to come. Pandemonium everywhere—on the inside out and the outside in. Cabinets con-

sumed with clutter. Clutter on all counters. We don't
know where to look.
Eyes dart, then settle. Focus on the caverns of the
cabinets before us. Kitchen knockoffs and knick-
knacks—rows of mugs, __14__, and __15___. I
catch a glimpse of my own reflection in the garden
window—the one that buckled then shattered this
week last year. An unexpected storm. Snow, then ice.
Too much weight. Now, the sun bounces off the re-
placement plexiglass. I see two eyes, a nose, a mouth.
Unrecognizable. They mock me, make motions as I
move. I know not whose mug I see. No matter, it's
time to cook dinner. Again.

TIME TO EAT

I asked for two pounds of chicken breasts, and they
delivered three pounds of thighs. I blame it on the
television. Magazines, too. Long legs covered in sheer
nylon beckon on front and back covers. The thighs
were on sale, *99 cents a pound*, he stated in a blunt
tone, devoid of lyrical quality or care, and dropped
the plastic bag full of substituted groceries on the
counter.
You get what you pay for, I replied, louder than intended,
then grabbed the knife and positioned the Kitchen
Aid. Secretly, I didn't mind the thighs. They always
have more flavor.
Personally, I've never understood the obsession with
body parts—neither as a practice of form or fashion.
It was the bargain hunting, body shaming, and
bounty swapping I'd had enough of. All of us con-
suming eye rolls, undercooked insults, and over-
cooked apologies for far too long. I unwrapped the
cellophane and dumped the whole lot, skin included,
into the pot of water. Chop celery. Slice carrots, Peel
potatoes. Pour, mix, stir gently. Boil off all imperfec-
tions and signs of scarring. Wait. Tempers boil. Soup,
too. Chicken stock pulses as hearts beat. Minutes

pass as moments accumulate. Hunger, too. Ulti-
mately, high heat turns to low. Settings neutralize.
Temperatures and tempers cool.
Dinner is served. Bon Appetit.

I NEED A NUMBER

Purchased yearly, as certain as seasons. An eight-by-five spiral packed with notes, names, and numbers. In a year marked by loss and longing, I tally and turn pages. Once forever friends, now strangers. I wonder how she is.

1. The color of Fall
2. Ice cream flavor
3. Type of pie
4. Backyard bird
5. Classic movie
6. Breakfast food (plural)
7. Classic board game
8. Casino card game
9. Top three/three top voting issues (each one word)

Hello, operator. I need a number—for a friend. I don't recall her address. Across town. Can you assist? She has __1_ eyes, prefers __2__ ice cream to __3___ pie, and sings like a ___4___. We've shared babies, bruised knees, and battered bodies. Tubs of

custard, chocolate covered raisins, and buttered pop-
corn. Nothing artificial. We've shared __5__, __6__
and __7__. Tested fate with __8__ and classic *Ouïja*.
Neither of us foresaw this future. Never did like *Sorry*.
Prefer strategy to games of chance. Hardboiled to
scrambled eggs. Felt to floppy slippers. Life, random.
Games of war everywhere. I apologize, Operator.
I'm rarely nostalgic. Not naïve, either. There are
miles and issues—___9___—between us. I miss her.
I'd like her number. Thank you, friend.

ON WOMAN'S DAY AND DAYS OF WONDER

Standing on the edge of the red kitchen tile, feet planted squarely on two rectangular hardwood planks, hands in the shape of triangles perched on each hip, I was advised to not leave trash in the garage. *Draws flies*, he said. *Really?*, I replied and returned his stare. Looked him in the eyes. *Good to know*. I picked up the monthly copy of *Woman's Day*. Rolled it into the shape of a cylinder
and swatted—hard—the fly buzzing just above his right shoulder. A small insect almost dusting—perhaps dancing—with the crisp cotton, freshly laundered. Of course. He frolics. I wash. Lilac and lemons. Freshly mowed grass. No. Stop. A direct hit. Clean. I've had practice. The fly dropped. A soft ping on the wood floor. An inch from the red tile. He continued to stare. I shrugged and tossed *Woman's Day* in the trash. Quickly pulled two red strips—limp until called to action—from the top of the plastic garbage bag and tied them in a knot. A basic bowline. Clean. Easy. Bow. I've had practice.
Take this to the garage, I said.
Still have no idea who pays for the magazine subscription. Only know it's not me.

I AM ALONE IN THE KITCHEN

It's 4 AM and I am alone in the kitchen. The others sleep—four on the floor above, two in the adjoining room, one in the cellar. They are of me and me of them. NPR whispers old news, the faucet drips, the heater hums, the dogs snore. I can taste the quiet and it's delicious. Like whipped buttercream filling, whoopie pies, melted brie on toast, chamomile tea. Inhale, exhale, consume, write. I am ravenous. Slow cooked pot roast, raspberry crème brulee, popcorn chicken. Inhale, exhale, consume, write. Strings of letters spill, syllables simmer, and words become phrases. I am insatiable. Shoulders drop and clenched fists unroll; unfamiliar hands wave back. *Greetings*, it's a pleasure to make your acquaintance. My belly rumbles, my toes curl, my nose twitches. I feel. I breathe. I am. The others sleep. I am of them and them of me. It's 7 AM and I am alone in the kitchen. I can taste the quiet. It's delicious.

ACKNOWLEDGMENTS

A version of "Blanks" first appeared in *A Catalyst Journal Vol. 1 Iss. 2* and *The Vital Sparks Vol. 2*
"Connective Tissue" and "In the Spirit of Stuff" first appeared in *Viral Imaginations: COVID-19*
"Things Called Mugs" first appeared in *Hive Avenue Literary Journal*
"Time to Eat" first appeared in *Nasty Women's Day Anthology--Moonstone Press*
"On Woman's Day and Days Spent Wondering" first appeared in *Love & the Pandemic—Moonstone Press*
"I am alone in the kitchen" first appeared in *Unstamatic Magazine Iss. April 2021*
A version of "I Need a Number" first appeared in *Snapdragon Journal Iss. 7.1*

To my teachers, mentors, and fellow learners, thank you for so generously sharing your love of words, craft, and life. I am forever grateful.

ABOUT THE POET

 Jen Schneider is an educator, attorney, and writer. She lives, writes, and works in small spaces throughout Philadelphia. She believes that everyone has a story and that all stories deserve to be shared. Her writing seeks to open space, voice, and heart with a goal of deeper understanding of both self and story. Her work explores daily experiences and interactions which reflect the fundamentally different and complex ways individuals live within, under, and through deeply entrenched systems. Her pieces create space for voice and variations in experiences that are inextricably intertwined with multiple identities and seek to capture the value inherent in those moments, often fleeting, where memory crystallizes in ways that yield new learning, heightened awareness, and deeper understanding. Choice of form is intentionally varied, with a goal of resisting categorizations as a matter of form and practice.

To learn more about Jennifer Schneider and discover more Next Chapter authors, visit our website at www.nextchapter.pub.

Invisible Ink
ISBN: 978-4-82412-495-1
Mass Market

Published by
Next Chapter
1-60-20 Minami-Otsuka
170-0005 Toshima-Ku, Tokyo
+818035793528

30th January 2022